Voynich Manuscript

An Illustrated Guide to the Perplexing Puzzles

(The True History of the Voynich Manuscript and Similar Works)

Lillie Berube

Published By **Oliver Leish**

Lillie Berube

Voynich Manuscript: An Illustrated Guide to the Perplexing Puzzles (The True History of the Voynich Manuscript and Similar Works)

ISBN 978-1-77485-609-3

No part of this guidebook shall be reproduced in any form without permission in writing from the publisher except in the case of brief quotations embodied in critical articles or reviews.

Legal & Disclaimer

The information contained in this ebook is not designed to replace or take the place of any form of medicine or professional medical advice. The information in this ebook has been provided for educational & entertainment purposes only.

The information contained in this book has been compiled from sources deemed reliable, and it is accurate to the best of the Author's knowledge; however, the Author cannot guarantee its accuracy and validity and cannot be held liable for any errors or omissions. Changes are periodically made to this book. You must consult your doctor or get professional medical advice before using any of the suggested remedies, techniques, or information in this book.

Upon using the information contained in this book, you agree to hold harmless the Author from and against any damages, costs, and expenses, including any legal fees potentially resulting from the application of any of the information provided by this guide. This disclaimer applies to any damages or injury caused by the use and application, whether directly or indirectly, of any advice or information presented, whether for breach of contract, tort, negligence, personal injury, criminal intent, or under any other cause of action.

You agree to accept all risks of using the information presented inside this book. You need to consult a professional medical practitioner in order to ensure you are both able and healthy enough to participate in this program.

Table Of Contents

introduction _________________________ 1

Chapter 1: Voynich And His Ugly Duckling
_________________________________ 3

Chapter 2: Skimming The Manuscript   19

Chapter 3: A Page In The Chapter On
Biology_______________________ 40

Chapter 4: A Representation Of Jacobus
De Tepenec ___________________ 50

Chapter 5: Currier Language A And B_ 91

Chapter 6: The Armadillo __________ 114

Chapter 7: First Folio_____________ 133

Chapter 8: The Drawings __________ 142

Introduction

"Yet it could be claimed that human ingenuity is unable to create a cipher that human ingenuity can't solve.

You may have recalled confiding with siblings about birthday parties, secret love affairs or other topics of hush-hush in front of their parents. They would then bewilder the parents with their fluency in Pig Latin. Other kids might recall writing bizarre vocabulary that was only accessible to them and their closest friends. This was especially useful when the teacher spotted one of their notes, as they were not able to embarrass note-passers when they couldn't comprehend the note.

On the other side in the range are military cryptographers, experts who earn their livelihood by in decoding and decoding the messages of the enemy. Whatever the level, mankind has always been fascinated by the idea of creating riddles and challenges that challenge the best minds of the world. In the same way, human beings are attracted by the desire to unravel the unsolvable, even to the point that for some, it could describe it as an addiction. One of the entities that put those curious minds against the wall - one that is like none other is the famous Voynich Manuscript.

Chapter 1: Voynich And His Ugly Duckling

Since the beginning of communication and language have been around humankind has been devising methods to hide their messages from the eyes of others. Officials from diplomatic and military organizations often develop secret codes for transmitting sensitive information and sensitive data to trusted individuals. This has become so widespread in recent years that entire fields of science, sports and professions that are fully-fledged are being developed to understand these mysterious texts, referred to as "cryptographers."

The earliest known evidence of the first cryptography evidence goes back to around the year 1907 BCE. Archaeologists were confused when they came upon an inscription in the eternal chamber of Khnumhotep II Khnumhotep

II, an Egyptian Aristocrat. Hieroglyphic symbols that have similar meanings, or a similarity of some kind could be used as substitutes for "ordinary" hieroglyphs. Although the intention was not to obscure the message, but rather elevate it, it has been described as the first attempt at "deliberate change in writing." Mesopotamians, Babylonians, Indians, Assyrians, Romans and almost every other civilization that was a powerhouse in antiquity also experimented with early technology.

In 5 BCE 5 BCE, the Spartans developed a cylindrical scroll-shaped device known as"the "Scytale," which allowed the Spartans to communicate their next actions and alerts of shifts in tactics and positions as well as other hidden messages, but without alerting enemies. The leather was thin, that were about the width of a tassel that was a part of the pom-pom of a cheerleader were woven around the Scytale with the text scribbled on the leather rings. It was categorized as an "transposition" encryption technique and the words written on the leather coils appeared absurd when they were unfurled, and they could only be solved by wrapping them around the Scytale that was the same size.

Naturally, the revolutionary techniques of cryptography, while dated and dated, are now considered to be archaic. The simple secrets of cryptography were made available to the public at large, and even integrated into kids' toys designed for aspiring spy. Since the majority of our society so dependent upon the internet, secrets have advanced to a completely new level, primarily by using data encryption. It seeks to hide classified electronic data through the use of sophisticated algorithms and ciphers were initially utilized to protect the military and government and is currently used as the principal method of security that the majority of websites (as as of

January 2017 at least 50%) provide to their users.

As complicated and complex as encryption of data may seem to us today there are a lot of clever and devious minds are finding ways to evade the most advanced encryption software and render any efforts made by huge teams that handle security on the internet ineffective. In actual fact the stories of unscrupulous hackers taking episodes from popular television shows and then threatening to release them prior to the release date and also reprobates stealing private photos of victims who have been harmed for ransom are becoming regular. While the government has a staff of full-time cryptanalysts specialized in retrieving encrypted information and decoding it to learn more about or deterring potential threats both from the inside and outside.

With such sharp minds working, one might be excused to believe that there are no cryptographic ciphers to be solved. However There is an array of contemporary and ancient cryptographic puzzles that have stumped even most experienced codebreakers of the present, as well as for the generations to be. The most well-known of these memorandums that are a mystery is one that dates back 600 years that still puzzles anyone who gazes on it, no matter if it's the first time or for the millionth time. It is the unique Voynich Manuscript.

To better understand the mystery which is known as the Voynich Manuscript, it is necessary to first look into his life as a intriguing person who came across the manuscript. Michal Habdank-Wojnicz, born on the night of All Hallows' Eve in 1865 in the current Lithuanian town of Telsiai. There isn't much information about his parents, aside of being born in Poland and of a noble family with some influence on the political scene during the turbulent Russian Empire. Michal liked his heritage and, as a teen He often signed documents under his alternate name, Wilfrid de Voynich, to display the blue veins in his blood.

Voynich

Prior to the age of six, Michal was relocated to the northwestern Polish community of Suwalki. There, he attended Suwalki's town's gimnazjum (junior high school) and attracted the attention of the teachers not just for his impressive grades, but also his preference for privacy. Instead of playing on playing with other kids, Michal would much rather lie down under the shade of a tree or hide in a corner, with his eyes set in an e-book.

Michal was evidently more privileged than the majority, as the evidence points to him being admitted to some of the top universities in Warsaw, St. Petersburg and Moscow toward the end of his childhood. It was in Moscow University that the board gave him a diploma as well as the degree of chemical chemistry. Soon after was when he obtained an authorization to practice as a pharmacist.

He worked in an apothecary, wearing a clean dark suit while he worked the counter, flanked by display cabinets and shelves that were filled with syrup bottles vibrant jars of herbs bottles of rare oils, herbal balms, and other such. However, it was soon apparent that while the static , sometimes monotonous task of dispensing powders and displacing liquids was all very well, there was no energy in his steps when he opened the at the beginning of each day.

Like many of the university-educated youngsters of his generation, Michal became both inspirited and passionate about the turbulent political situation in Poland in the midst of. In 1885, the 20-year-old returned to the city of one of his alma maters, Warsaw, and enlisted in the socialist sympathizer Ludwik Warynski's workers' party, the "Proletarjat." Michal was also known to be a vehement supporter of Sergey Stepnyak-Kravchinsky, a Ukrainian revolutionary with democratic ideals who often preached to the peasant classes and incited insurgencies against autocratic rule, namely Tsar Alexander II of Russia.

Sergey Stepnyak-Kravchinsky

The following year, Michal attempted to free the two conspirators in prison, Stanislaw Kunicki and Piotr Bardowski, two fighters for national liberation , who had been sent to the gallows in the Warsaw Citadel for their alleged plots against the authorities. The problem was that Michal got nabbed during the course of proceedings by Russian officials after an "police spy" identified him to authorities. All other rebels were executed, while the flailing and thrashing Michal was put in an unsanitary cell and put in solitary confinement within the basement of the citadel, escaped due to his nobility. It's unclear the length of time Michal was held for but it was enough to cause him to be suffering from tuberculosis as well as a permanent slumped back.

Michal was eventually able to slip out of the cell and then shortly thereafter he regrouped from where he was and began his anti-autocracy work with the fire that was shining brighter than ever before. Unfortunately, the authorities once again came after Michal, but this time they punished Michal with a lifetime of work at his Siberian salt mines in Tunka.

Michal could be as slippery and quite smooth and, in the end, he was able to slip away from authorities again. The wounds that he suffered after narrowly escaping his captors as badges of honour. In later years the man would take off his shirt for people who wanted to know about his experiences in his previous life. Then, he explained the three injuries on his torso. "Here I have an axe," he said. "Here is a weapon and I've got an arrow."

After escaping from the guards of the salt mines Michal drove to the city of Irkutsk in which he was sheltered at the home of Karauloff family members. Karauloff family. After eating him and providing the guest an energizing shower as well as food and a meal, the Karauloffs encouraged him to leave all connections with Russia and beginning afresh in England. Before sending him off, the Karauloffs inserted a slip of paper with Stepnyak-Kravchinsky's name and London address into the small satchel they had packed for him. The name of Stepnyak was listed. specifics of a "Lily Boole,"" who was better known under her maiden name in full, "Ethel Lilian Boole." She would later become Michal's future spouse.

Due to the numerous mishaps that befell Michal during his travels and it was quite a shock that he managed to reach

London in intact. The man walked to the west and stopped in Hamburg in the middle of nowhere, hiding from view in unlocked stables. The food items in his satchel had been thrown away, Michael pulled his belt tighter and made a living off scraps. Michael eventually was able to get his glasses as well as the expensive coat, which was muddy and dirty, off his back and was able to secure an entry ticket for 3rd class on a fruit boat bound to England and also some herring and bread. In early 1890, a dehydrated and malnourished Michal, who spoke not a lick of English, finally set foot on the London docks, and from there, he wasted no time in tracking down Stepnyak-Kravchinsky.

Following the guidance from Richard Garnett, the "Keeper of Printed Books" at the British Museum, Michal began to explore books from the past. This intrigued him because of a variety of reasons. Fluency in English wasn't a prerequisite for the position, and it allowed him to travel the globe to find books that were both rare and "lost" books that can then be sold to readers back in London for a hefty price. These books that have been lost, especially ones that date back to in the sixteenth century are called "incunabula."

in 1898 Michal formed a company partnership along together with Charles Edgell, another ambitious Cambridge graduate. Together they published the first catalog. His first catalogue was an enormous success and the shrewd Michal who had spotted the golden goose set up his first store in 1 Soho Square two years after. The very year, Michal released his second catalogue that received more praise than his first. A lot of people in the region were credited with igniting the new trend of Londoners pushing each other away from the street to acquire the unique prints. The year 1902 was the time that Michal as well as Ethel got married. By 1904, he was granted the British citizenship. From that point onward he officially adopted the name Wilfrid Michael. Voynich.

Voynich transformed from an emerging talent into a force to be reckoned with. He earned an excellent reputation for his unwavering intuition and a keen eye that appeared to be able to spot the most rare of spots. His English increased dramatically with time and his arsenal of multilingual language skills grew due to his frequent travels. Despite his success He remained humble and remained so at least during the early days of his professional career. According to one of his staff in the bookshop "He was fluent in 18 languages, and all, according to him equally poorly."

At some point, Voynich's ambitions increased, to the point that he forgot his values in the in the name of business. In Italy the country that was among his most favorite areas to mine for the literary gold mine, he bought numerous reams and reams of manuscripts from churches. In the end, he admitted that on one of his purchases that took him to a convent that was homely in rural Italy He was able convincing the nuns their library was full of obsolete books and "dusty garbage." Actually the convent was having a stash of old printed books and codices that were worth many thousands lire. In just a few months, Voynich had made off from the convent's books and then returned with according to his own words, boxes of "modern rubbish." A second trip to Corsica was where he robbed the local church of as many as 600 prints.

In 1912, Voynich came across the biggest and most important discovery of his professional career. When he learned that Villa Mondragone, owned by the Jesuits Mondragone was preparing to liquidate the assets of its owners, he made the trip towards Frascati in the Italian city of Frascati to have a look at the state of affairs. While he sifted through the more than 300 covers that were strewn across the floors and tables of the library and handled these important volumes with extra caution, a mysterious chest at the corner attracted his interest. He made his way to the chest, loosened the lock that was rusty and when he pulled the door open his eyes feasted on a selection of books that were unmarked. From the chest, Voynich selected another 30 prints to add to his growing collection.

In the middle of the prints was an unappealing, loosely bound stack of papers, which he might have ignored had not it been the vividly colored illustrations as well as the notes that were scribbled on the margins that gave him insight to the text's historical significance and its potential value. He was grateful to his lucky stars when he went back to his bookshop to examine the manuscript using the appropriate equipment, as it was then that he realized that he'd found the ultimate prize. A passage from the diary of

Voynich in the evening hints at his joy: "It was such an ugly duckling when compared to the others, with its elaborate decorations and gold colors...My curiosity was sparked immediately ...[whenI discovered the entire text was written in the cipher."

A page of the manuscript

Chapter 2: Skimming The Manuscript

"Well surely, it is true that the Voynich Manuscript can be described as the "limit text for Western occultism. It is not accessible to anyone. It's an obsequious book." -- Terrence McKenna late 20th-century American ethnobotanist

According to the account from E. Millicent Sowerby, one of the clerks hired just after the purchase of the manuscript the bookshop was regularly overrun by suspicious customers Voynich declared "spies." The spy-like individuals, who posed in the role of customers frequently visit the bookshop and, while they appeared friendly enough to be approached however, they did not actually purchase anything. Instead, they sat on the sidelines , as they sat in the corner and their eyes were focused on the every move of Voynich. Initially, Sowerby chalked them up to be nothing more than ambitious entrepreneurs who were hoping to build an enduring business connection with the famous book retailer, but as the strangers who were threatening continued to display their smug faces and snarl, his alarm bells set. Could they could be spies working for Voynich's lusty rivals, or could they be seeking something particular which they knew had made it's way into the hands of Voynich? If the former is the case, what is it that was appealing about this mysterious codex?

The particular codex measured roughly 8.9 and 6.3 inches. It was made entirely of Vellum (parchment composed of goat or calf skin) and was used from the book's cover to its 240 pages from which only 116 pages have been identified. Its contents were split by later owners into 6 chapters -horticultural, astronomical, cosmological, biological/balneological, pharmaceutical, and recipes. The fragile vellum cover barely hanging on to its hinges after it arrived at Voynich and is now believed to date to the 18th century or early 19th century and is believed to be substituted by its prior Jesuit owners, as covers in a similar fashion were frequently discovered throughout Roman Jesuit libraries. The cover, which was not marked, had no name or author the cover was later named by the person who first discovered the manuscript, and remains ascribed to by the name of Voynich Manuscript.

The most prominent and distinct characteristic of this manuscript evidently it's the beautiful written in calligraphy, but completely unintelligible text that every single word was written in. Experts have found that the scattered fragments of Latin writing that was found in the margins was added later by the owner. Although there is no punctuation marks separating the 170,000 glyphs, which isn't that are found in any language anyway - the text was broken into shorter paragraphs and in line with Western practices, appeared to be composed from right to left, line-by-line. This is why people speculate that a bizarre "word" comprised of what appears to be a figure-8 that is followed by a quick scrawl, with a curlicue could be the author's method of signalling a stop for breath. The most puzzling part was the lack of any erasure marks or any overlapping glyphs to be observed or indicate that the writer had been extremely cautious in the execution or that he she, or they been pounding out the text in a lengthy, "supernatural" trance.

Another distinctive feature in the text was the rainbow of illustrations and sketches with varying sizes, including some of them so tiny that one needed to look up to see them , and others that were so big they filled entire pages and even some foldouts. These drawings were, in many cases, able to jump right off the pages because of their extremeness seemed to be some kind of medieval or science reference book at first glance. On second inspection you may be puzzled by the striking contrast between the drawings. The full-color illustrations appear to have been created with the kind of precision you would only find by the best of medieval artists, however they were also surrounded by the kind of drawings that can be described as unprofessional and sketchy drawings, some partially, while others were totally non-colored. The drawings of the second type aside from looking like unplanned afterthoughts, looked childish, like they were made by a different hand.

Pages from the manuscript , with illustrations in various sizes

While there are plenty possibilities, they aren't any absolute answers to the question of who the person who wrote the manuscript or at the least the person who illustrated this work was. However, the paint's ingredients and the color palette, have offered some clues which have enabled people to build a sketchy picture. In the 15th century Europe as among the more well-known dates that are connected to the author of the manuscript the color inks were expensive. The process of creating these colors was an "technical problem" and an art in its own way, requiring years of experience and knowledge. The larger crystals and minerals typically created the most vibrant hues however mixing them was an exhausting process because their heft and rough texture make it difficult to crush and put them on canvas. Renaissance artists were able to explore a whole new range of colors thanks to the new materials available , making use of ultramarine, azurite, and indigo, to create breathtaking shades of blue, as well as glowing green hues by combining verdigris, malachite as well as green earth. Whites, browns, blacks and other neutral shades were generally used by those in the upper and middle echelons of society because they were made of easily available materials, like bone char, umber (crushed bones of animals) and gypsum stones and bone char.

The colors utilized throughout the text, especially in the horticultural section that featured flashes of green, brown blue, and even a splash of yellow and red, however, these colors were significantly duller than paints that cost more at the day. For these reasons, it is believed it is believed that the author came from a low-income background, with a limited budget and the manuscript relied heavily on greens and browns to brighten the illustrations. However the paint used that was used in the text - with sloppy sketches aside it was uniformly applied to the point that, even after time, the consistent color, even though slightly faded, has remained within the guidelines.

The horticultural portion in the text is by far the most lengthy of sections, comprising hand-drawn drawings of 126 that fill 130 pages. While the text seemed to be nothing more than a scribbled gibberish anyone who was able to read it could recognize that the manuscript's section on horticulture, as the title suggests, was full of herbs and plants. Any other information would be pure speculation.

The drawings may have the characteristics of a conventional plant However, the majority - - a theme that is present throughout the Codex - had the same traits as well-known plants, even though they were distinctive enough that botanists have discovered it nearly impossible to categorize the plants. If these plants were actually present at some point the past, it, according to some could indicate that these plants were only revealed to the author of the manuscript, possibly by a higher authority.

The horticultural illustrations were evidently drawn prior to the addition of text since the writer wrote meticulously around their art work, a method used by a number of Renaissance artists. However, unlike artists of the time who frequently reused their designs especially when it was related to plants and flowers however, the artwork found in the manuscript has been seen in any of the prior literature or in the reverse direction. While the plants in the manuscript were, they were not sufficiently distinct enough for people to draw connections - some more uncertain and some more definitive - among the existing plants and these wacky plants. In addition, by humouring the labels, one may be able trace the author's roots or at most, where his travels were taking his journey.

For instance On Folio 32R, there's an entire page of illustrations depicting the "upright plant" that has multiple levels of branches that are adorned sparsely with an elliptical shape of leaflets of moss-green. Each branch was decorated by white flowers, reminiscent of popcorn kernels that were fluffy and sprinkled with indigo blues and beiges. A few have also pointed out similarities between the plant and thunbergia grandiflora, which is also called"the "sky flowers." Mostly located in India the plant had a similar arrangement of leaves with the same hue, however they were heart-shaped, not an elliptical shape, and also "clusters of white or light blue flowering tubulars."

If this plant really was the one that soared in the sky then the Italian author had to have traveled extensively and this would be in direct contradiction to the idea of its creator having less fortunate backgrounds. It could also suggest that the writer was from India or that this plant, as well as other plants in the manuscript, had been conceived only in their minds. But the plant's link with the flower of the night has been cut off by a team of expert horticulturists who pointed to the fact that this Indian plant does not possess the distinctive stamens or pistols protruding from the flowering plants in the manuscript's.

In recent times, other researchers have been able to suggest that the manuscript has connection to the Americas and the codex format dates is from the 16th century of Mexico. Rexford Talbert and Arthur Tucker from Delaware State University compared the xiuhamolli commonly referred to by the name of "soap plant" discovered in 1552 Codex Cruz-Badianus (or "Aztec Herbal") with another from the Voynich plants. Both were characterized by "broad white-to-gray" caudices (thick trunk-like stems of woody plants) as well as bumpy bark and toenail-like root systems. The researchers later discussed what they observed in their journal "The depictions of the two Mesoamerican creatures are so similar, they could be painted by the exact same person or group or group of artists."

A different Voynich plant, or as the researchers say, has striking resemblances to the "viola tricolore of Eurasia," a special kind of flower with five petals that has violet, yellow and white ombre, which is common within North America. In addition to six animals and one mineral, the team identified 37 other of the 303 distinct plants and flowers that adorned on the page of this manuscript. They also identified 37 other unique flowers and greenery with the origins of Texas, California, Nicaragua and many more.

In 1944, another renowned botanist at the Catholic University of America named Hugh O'Neill made new waves in the field when he claimed that he had successfully identified the plant in Folio F33V. The plant was unique, and included spiky tubers, leaves that resembled stars and a flat, yellow disc that appeared to be an "seed bed" covered with immaculately intricate "purple-black" petals that were edged with white, O'Neill claimed that it was the sunflower. Because this plant was introduced to Europe after Columbus his voyages towards North America, he hoped to pin down the date of its origin to the 1500s. In the end, at the conclusion of the day, O'Neill's idea, like the many theories published before and after it was just a speculative guess.

The chapters on cosmology and astrology which followed were as complicated and ambiguous like their horticultural counterparts. The pages of the chapter on astrology contain intricate illustrations, with images of the moon, sun, and the uncanny constellations of stars within its central area. The majority of these pictures were accompanied by short text that appeared to be author's labels for these pages.

The chapters on cosmology and astronomy are often discussed in conjunction by cryptographers. However, 12 pages of drawings based on the zodiac are usually classified under the chapter on astrology. The pages of cosmology however are adorned with intricate circular designs. A lot of them were wheels, and some were cut into three-crusted cakes, with star-shaped arrangements and awe-inspiring symbols that are associated with the seasons of a Western calendar and zodiac and winds patterns.

The most interesting aspect of the chapter on cosmology was the foldout of six pages which when laid out to the fullest extent it showed nine connected circles The largest was placed at the in the center on the paper. The circles, decorated with geometric scales as well as different designs that were distinctive, but also complementary were adorned with minimalist sketches of castles that popped at them from the sides. The center circle contained a collection of six towers, surrounded by a lake of stars with onion-shaped domes as well as decorative stems, topped by clover-like pendants.

With the aid of an magnifying glass with a magnifying glass, one might also be able to discern the tiny, faded image of a tower. could be interpreted as evidence of the existence of a "transfer," whereas others dismiss it as simply an unintentional dust smudge. It is referred to by cryptographers as the "Rosettes" page and its presence of castles that are drawn in rough sketch have led to many believing that it was an actual map. Self-professed cryptographers and Internet investigators have decided to mark these circles with kingdoms that they could have represented. For instance, the central part of example is believed to be a hint of "Russia's Golden Circle," and the peppermint swirl of a circle beneath it, with blue and red dots, is the "Black Sea."

The chapter on the zodiac, a intriguing section that is found in this manuscript has characters reminiscent of those found in ancient astrology, but on closer examination, they appear to represent the constellations and signs that are based on the traditions of a different time or, as some claim, an entirely different world. The average thirty naked "nymphs" carrying "star-shaped flowers" as well as the emblem of the zodiac symbol it represented, were contained within the huge "concentric circle" of the zodiac wheels of the manuscript. Cryptographers who are observant have noticed two kinds of ink found that are used in this chapter. The written script that was scratched underneath the zodiac significations was not just written with darker ink but was clearly written by an entirely different hand. Furthermore, in contrast to the standard zodiac, the one depicted in the manuscript didn't begin with Aries and ended started with Pisces. The zodiac wheels dedicated to Capricorn and Aquarius have since been ripped off the pages of the document and have been lost to the hand of time. Additionally, there are those who believe that the wheels, along with the other pages that are missing from the manuscript, were deliberately torn out by those who were unable to allow a second set of eyes to examine their contents, as they could contain secrets that are too important to be shared with the world.

The crest that was in the middle of the Pisces wheel was an extremely poorly painted, non-colored fish that had an apex that was pointed, and it was accompanied by"Mars, "Mars," the French word meaning "March." The text is vital to remember that the "a" that is found in the script, which may be a little skewed is identical to the As seen on other labels in the manuscript, which indicates that these labels were written by the same person. It was only natural that the decoder begin with the astrological part because it had the most obvious and solely - similarity to the world as it is.

Its Aries wheel, depicted with just 15 nymphs was centered by a menially drawn ram that was gray. It was behind it was a tree, which resembled the hand and arm of a deformed man that emerged from the grass in front of it. The two were drab colored and had the appearance of blotches of green. A few researchers have shed light on the similarities of the manuscript's main ram as well as the ram of the Codex Schurstab, a German "treatise on medical astrology" that was published around the time of the 15th century. the latter with an almost identical background however, most agree that this general resemblance to the manuscript is a bit of a stretch.

The wheel that followed the Taurus and the fact that it also contained 15 nymphs. It is evident that the author of the manuscript had no experience in the design of animals and animals generally. The bull on the symbol of the wheel as well as other of the animals in the manuscript included a crooked hind leg and were disproportionately proportioned many of them having necks that were too small to support heads of this size. More generously painted in striking brick red the bull is shown slopping the water out of the bucket.

A unique twist to the zodiac of the manuscript was its representation of Gemini. Twins from The Gemini wheel, in contrast to their typical depictions, were depicted as fraternal twins from opposite genders. One could be thinking about, since there could have been some reason why the writer chose to dress the brothers with a male green tunic with a matching beret-like hat, as well as the woman in a gorgeous indigo dress , amidst the sea of naked Nymphs that were scattered across the manuscript.

Another thing that chin-scratches the astrological chapter is the three crowns that are worn by central nymphs on the Cancer, Leo, and Libra wheels. All crowns are white except for the crown of the nymph Leo that is brightened by a dab of royal red. Numerous zodiac nymphs are also sporting "tressed" hairstyles and braided hairstyles. Others believe the squiggles could be flowers or wreaths. What really places the zodiac wheels onto a level when compared to other enthralling illustrations in the text is the author's claim to have used "primeval animated." If these wheels were turned in a way, they could make a stunning illusion of an endless the naked nymphs each carrying their own stars-flowers.

The following section, dubbed the balneological or biochemical (referring towards baths and baths or) section, can be usually highlighted as being the one most "unusual" part in the text. It's a feast of text with a slender wall of text and is punctuated by scattered appearances of skinny-dipping nymphs like sisters to those of the astrological portion - and others with oddities as well as a serpentine web of pipes, bathing pools that are communal and platforms made from clouds.

Chapter 3: A Page In The Chapter On Biology

As with every other part of the manuscript regardless of size or tiny, cryptographers have meticulously studied these amazing drawings and, consequently, they've developed their personal interpretations of the issue. Some say that the drawings depict the shocking rituals that were performed by some ancient secret society or cult However, the majority cryptographers are convinced of the possibility that they are more symbolic than real. Some have discovered some metaphors in the image that are related with "alchemical" or "natural" process. Others prefer to put their attention to illustrations of miniature bathing nymphs wallowing in the pools (pictured sporting healthy and round abdomens) engaging and playing with the bizarre capsules and tubes.

Some have drawn connections between the manuscript's bizarre green baths and the pool that were featured in Balneis Puteolanis, an thirteenth century Roman poem that focused on the therapeutic benefits of spa waters , others believe that the text held some of the mysteries of the fountain of youth. and more specifically that of Der Jungbrunnen. Oil paintings, which is a masterpiece by The German Renaissance painter Lucas Cranach the Elder depicted the pool of young ladies splashing about in gray water. To the left of the pool is the women drying off. In front of them was a tent, where naked women entered and from the opposite part of the red blood curtain, left, dressed and with a children. But, unlike the maidens of Cranach, who appeared to be a replica from the woman who was in her the nymphs of the manuscript, though much less sophisticated, were depicted with distinctive facial characteristics and expressions. Their sexy bosoms and absence of wrinklesthat some believe is a connection to the fountain that nourishes youth is probably a coincidence.

The most cogent of all these balneological-related theories often juxtaposes its images with bodily organs, its most glaring hint being the pipes, tubes, and capsules, which were drawn almost to resemble blood vessels and arteries. The tube-like borders that are running between the left and top sides of the Folio is a good example. It is coupled by a nymph who showers with water cascading down on her from the pipe above it is believed to be a representation of the aorta. The other Nymphs showering themselves with vessels that resemble aliens are a reference to the heart as well as heart and the "4 humorous aspects of hippocratic Medicine - Yellow bile (fire) and the black bile (earth) and the phlegm (water) as well as blood (air)."

The nymphs were enjoying themselves within the pipes that flanked Folio77V and included an ankle-deep maiden in her own water pool with her arms stretched out and her hand shoved into the pipe openings either side of her are believed to symbolize an anatomy for the intestinal tract as well as the appendix.

The Nymphs of the section on biology were depicted with crowns, however only one is seen with what could be a cross or something like the cross-staff-hybrid cross that St. John the Baptist is often depicted carrying. The cross alone was enough to spark theories about obscure Christian symbols, however these theorists may be looking at the manuscript, as it is not just brimming with cosmology, astrology and other pagan phenomenon, but the cross appears to be the only tangible symbol of the religion found in this entire document.

Not last are the pharmaceutical and recipes chapters that constitute the final pages of the manuscript that is evasive. Within these sections, one is likely to discover a series of medical instructions that seem to focus on the treatment of unknown ailments as well as recipes for all kinds of bizarre brews and strange potions. The botanical illustrations and other sketches tucked in between the awe-inspiring text were intended to help describe the herbal guidelines and formulas for healing however some of them are so odd that they actually accomplish the opposite.

The chapter on drugs in the manuscript is contained in three bifolios. They were two sheets that were folded to form four segments that were all folded out. The right-hand part of every segment was allocated to a mix of leaves, roots and petals or "fragments" from medicinal plants arranged on neatly laid out rows of around 1 to 9 per and the brief stanzas of text below the fragments. The remaining portion of the segment - which was actually more of a margin, as it was only one fifth of the entire page was reserved for 3-4 so-called "containers," amounting to 45 total. The people who have looked over this manuscript may have wondered whether this chapter of the codex was not completed by the author since some labels seem to be absent in the spare pages.

Although they looked like badly proportioned wedding cakes as well as towers of bongo drums the majority of people have concluded that the containers to be extravagant containers for apothecary that have multiple levels. The containers, as cryptographers believe they are treens, the name refers to tiny trinkets as well as household objects that are carved from wood. The Voynich containers could be "turned over, carved," and then licked with a glimmer of paint. These unusual containers were used to store herbs, powders and drops of medicinal.

Some have noticed a kinship between Voynich containers as well as the apothecary vessels that were made during the medieval period of Europe. A good example is the apparatuses within "page 99 verso" an elongated pillar that is adorned by orange, red, blue and blue patterns. The pillar has been compared to a wooden sewing case dating from the 19th century France which was designed as a pepper mill that could be turned open in order to place their needlework tools in the velvet-lined compartment. Another brown Voynich container, with a needle sticking out of its bulbous head, and positioned against what appears to be the root of a turnip with stripes, is compared to the Austrian necessaire made of wood, another sewing case. There are other Voynich vessels are believed to have a similar style and design as Egyptian perfume bottles and ones with feet, to herbal jars that were made in Norway.

Near the end of the manuscript, there is a recipes chapter, consisting of only passages that were separated with "tail-less" stars that had seven or eight points, each highlighted with red, yellow and black dots in the middle.

Other than the ornamental rings, tiaras flasks, spindles, cannabis leaves, and various other real world objects that were spotted by decoders are the odd animals found within the text. One of the more bizarre animals was the tiny non-colored silhouette of the dragon that was found in the chapter on horticulture, eating on a massive 16-sided leaf that was several times its size.

Other famous animals include snakes, birds, goats, frogs, as well as sheep. Also, there was an animal with an elongated, padded back and long snoutthat some believe is the pangolin that is typically seen in Africa.

Again, it should be noted that the connections mentioned above are just speculation. However, even if one of these theories had some merit however, there are numerous Voynich components that are not bound by any designation with absolute certainty.

Three Magi and the King

"Cut the Sonne in three pieces, that's how Nature has made and then strengthen it all by itself and you can cut off the powders of Sonne into twine, for a duration and make the wound heal again. ..." -- Testamentum Johannis The Dee Philosophia Summi in Johannem Gwynn

As the story goes, a few months after Voynich's discovery of the manuscript, the pharmacist-turned-book dealer came across yet another happy accident. One day, as he was working on a set of photos in the darkroom he installed at the back of his bookshop, he fell over a bottle of chemical for photo-developing by bending his elbow. He swiftly snatched the manuscript from the table however the damage was already done. He immediately took a dry cloth to wipe up the mess he'd created however, before he could clean the liquid from the the manuscript's first page his eyes were narrowed to the fine writing that was appearing right in front of his very eyes. He gently blew air on the damp surface and then fanned it using his fingers until the four words were crystallized. He spoke the words repeatedly and over again, his ears ringing in excitement. Jacobus de Tepenec and beneath it, the shorter but not revealing abbreviation for four letters, "Prag."

Chapter 4: A Representation Of Jacobus

De Tepenec

Naturally, the discovery of Tepenec's name is in various versions. Some claim that the splotch in one of the manuscripts was result of a regrettable, yet deliberate effort on the part of Voynich as he was aware of the name a few days earlier and had dabbed the area with special chemicals in intention of making the letters more attractive. Some say that he'd tried to create an "photostatic replica" (a photographic copy) from the original manuscript to be used for review purposes and instead, he uncovered an earlier-hidden name due to the unexposed plate.

Voynich isn't the only person to alter the manuscript. The chapter on gardening is particularly battered, and its pages are brimming with holes, surrounded by brown edges. The burn marks are believed that they are the results of the past cryptographers equipped with droppers of lemon juice, trying to find hidden messages written in ink that was invisible.

However, the name of Tepenec sufficed to start the official record of ownership, which allowed historians to follow its progress. After conducting a series of investigations, Tepenec was bumped up to the second spot on the list. His name replaced by the name of Holy Roman Emperor Rudolf II. Rudolf II, later nicknamed "the Mad Alchemist" by his peers was a gifted scholar and was fascinated by literature, science, mathematics and alchemy. He was proficient of Spanish, French, German, Italian, Latin, and also conversational Czech that was great to entertain foreign diplomats and the monarchs in royal banquets, gatherings and banquets.

Rudolf II

As it is claimed, money doesn't make everything. The Emperor was troubled and was often prone to moody moods, episodes of depression, and various mental disorders, which were only able to worsen in a more rapid manner as he gained the position of. In 1577, a young Rudolf was struck by the first of an array of anxiety attacks and nervous breakdowns. He finally reached the point where it was difficult for him to leave his castle.

In 1580, he had barely more than bones and skin and had fallen into such a miserable condition that his friends began to worry about his future. While he slowly managed to recover the weight he dropped, his falling spirits were not yet raised. If his paranoia was unchecked, it was clear that assassins was preparing to attack him. He was not a believer in anyone particularly not his family members who's hands were aching to get his crown. The treasure chests and gold were secured with padlocks and kept at the bedside at all times. When he began to develop doubts about his staff he even took out the castle's pantries to show them the lesson.

To ensure being healthy, around 1583 Rudolf decided to get rid of himself from the chaos of Vienna and establish a his permanent home at Prague's Bohemia. To keep himself from his mood swings In order to keep himself secluded in the library of the castle for hours at a time and absorbed alchemical, astronomical and paranormal literature from cover book. He built collecting occult items by purchasing exclusive artifacts as well as texts. Many of them were offered to him as being the only collection of their kind. He dispersed his government officials and diplomats in favor of a more private and intimate environment. He would surround himself with an elite group of astronomers, artists artisans, antiquarians and scholars from all over the globe.

Rudolf did not pay attention to the political chaos and let the turmoil to simmer at the back of his mind. The emperor believed that the many unexplored avenues for exploration in the exciting techniques of alchemy as well as "scientific" magic demanded more focus.

It is not surprising that the emperor's enthusiasm for unconventional science attracted as many as if not more - skeptics and fraudsters as academics with a stellar record The second group included the highly regarded German Astrologer Johannes Kepler.

In this time of the emperor's obsession with strange science, believed to have occurred between the years 1610 and 1610, when Rudolf bought the Voynich Manuscript from a shady seller for an astronomical amount in the amount of 600 ducats (roughly $86,250 in the present) The officials of the emperor were utterly dissatisfied by his impulsive and extravagant purchase which was most likely taken from an unidentified place in Italy as well. When they discovered that the emperor had bought a book nobody could even read and the colour of their complexions would have certainly drained more quickly.

But who was Jacobus de Tepenec, and how did the manuscript come to being within his hands? Jacobus was an Moravian native "Jakub Horcicky" was raised in a blue collar family. As the family struggled to scrape enough, he landed the position of kitchen aide in an academy run by Jesuits in Krumlov however, he did not be able to receive an education in the formal sense until he was admitted to the Krumlov Seminary which was an institution for children who were poor aged 15. Beginning that year, 1590, the hardworking young man began a new part-time job as an assistant at the college pharmacy. He diligently shadowed his boss who was the Bohemian pharmacy Dr. Martin

Schaffner and was able to develop an interest in the profession.

After graduating from the gimnazjum, Jacobus was granted a license, and began to practice the trade by himself, surviving on a modest but adequate income for a few years. In 1598 Jacobus was hoping to increase his knowledge about the profession he was pursuing, relocated to Prague and went back to school. He was a student of the philosophy of Aristotle. Alongside studying, Jacobus juggled both chemical and pharmaceutical jobs in the background.

Once he was able to be able to, Jacobus rented out a warehouse in Schimov, a nearby village Prague and then converted it into a lab could be his own. There, he set up and harvested his very own herbs garden, and also played around with a range of alcohols that was infused with herbs, ultimately the launch of the brand of his own healing drinks and rejuvenating drinks. With the help of top-of-the-line marketing, the bottles began to sell out of the shelf, often much faster than they could replenish the shelves.

His most famous product was Aqua Sinapis (derived from his Latin surname Sinapius) that was made using distillation to create a crystal clear kind of alcohol before injecting it with extracts from mustard seeds. Alongside his impressive selling skills, Jacobus impressed local scholars by inventing a method that could "transfer the aroma of flowers" to a liquid form. He was believed to have cooked up the first batch of modern day perfumes.

In the wake of his money, he began to meet with top-ranking officials from the political sphere In time, he was acquainted with the Emperor Rudolf II. He was a key contributor to financing some of Rudolf's alchemical endeavors and paid off many of his obligations. In return, he was later awarded with a property located in Melnik.

The year 1607 was the one when Jacobus became the "Imperial Chemist" of Rudolf's court but he also went under the names to "Chief Botanist" and "Imperial Distiller" in addition to many other titles. In 1607, Jacobus was summoned to Rudolf's castle. The emperor, who was suffering from another debilitating bout of depression, refused to seek traditional help, and instead hired the pharmaceutical/botanical expert as his personal psychiatrist. This is how Jacobus began a strict regime that included Aqua Sinapus, other herbal extracts and teas that were specially formulated, that supposedly worked miracles. To make sure that his claims were in line against Jacobus, Rudolf ennobled him in the year he was born, awarding his the name "de Tepenec" and thrusting at him an array of gifts, including the invaluable Voynich Manuscript. Soon after receiving the codex Jacobus was, as other people, seemed confused by the value of it - opened the book and signed his name on the upper right-hand corner on the front page.

Other cryptographers agree that Rudolf who was a zealous fan of the unknown, never given up the manuscript whether by choice or through force, particularly given the amount of gold he was forced to pay to purchase it. They believe the emperor was only temporarily granted it to Jacobus and requested Jacobus to translate its message. Maybe it was the emperor who given instructions to Jacobus to sign his name on the manuscript so that should it be lost, it would be returned to him.

It raises another issue why the emperor would use only one cryptographer for complete the task, instead of distribute it to ensure to be subjected to the scrutiny of several individuals? There is a theory that Rudolf was shrewd enough to believe that the language of the manuscript contained supernatural and alchemical secrets. In the context of the hostile environment at the time, caused through an era of Christian persecution of the heresies and "devil-worshiping sorcerers" These were the exact science that the Church worked hard to eradicate, which means that Rudolf was likely to have felt the need to keep trying at decoding the secrets.

The historians of today are fairly certain that the book was not in mint in the year it was in Rudolf's possession. Unfortunately any clues that may provide clues to the person who wrote it are either difficult dead ends or more unanswered inquiries and weak postulations. Did the manuscript truly represent an ancient treasure found in a distant country, or could it be the work of a group of conniving, calculated criminals?

Although it was more prudent to keep his love of the occult hidden The news of Rudolf's astonishing private collection spread quickly, especially in the circles of trader and merchants. In addition the emperor wasn't very a shrewd shopper, and was known to pay an attractive sum on anything that caught his interest at any moment. In the end, swindlers were abounding in the castle, selling their useless potions or fake artifacts and possibly even a meaningless book composed of random squiggles. One that was so captivating that it has been able to fool millions of people throughout the years.

The top possible suspects were a well-known pair of self-proclaimed alchemists, wizards and psychics with name of Sir Edward Kelley and John Dee. Before Kelley embarked on a journey into the world of the paranormal it was his job to be the scribe in his home town in Worcester, England. He worked for a long time in the same job until he was fired abruptly for smuggling official documents. There is a rumor that his ear was cut off in the course of his crimes. He kept secret from potential clients by wearing a variety of hairstyles for long hair, wigs and huge caps.

Kelley

Disappointed from the humiliating dismissal and without a direction to go, Kelley transformed himself to become a spirit medium and occult expert in a matter of minutes. Kelley might have had to work hard in order to learn how to communicate however should there be something that was his birthright smooth, slurred speech and artistically crafted ways that allowed Kelley to draw an audience of new people in no time. The year 1582 was when Kelley was introduced to a smart and entrepreneur mathematician called John Dee. Dee who was desperately seeking a medium, or crystal-gazer who could communicate with angels, was thrilled when Kelley said he had met his match. Kelley clearly won his trust within a single session and he was Dee's personal scryer after that. Between 1582-1589 The "blessed" couple performed hundreds of spiritual readings as well as "prayers for spiritual awakening" across the nation.

Kelley might not have been the best However, if there was something that can be denied, it's his ability to be as smart in business and an ingenuous mind. In addition, he knew precisely how to attract his public. In the trip to Wales in the year just one year into his relationship and Dee, Kelley managed to acquire the world's sole copy of The Book of Saint Dunstan which was an alchemical workbook that was said to teach one how to transform special white and red powders to metals. In the following weeks, Kelley presented Dee with "2 ivory caskets" packed with samples of powders. They claimed that he was believed to have been led to by an "spiritual entity." Kelley was then able to spend the next couple of days in the lab that he set up in the kitchen. Later, he was appearing with 3 sparkling golden nuggets that was given to Dee and two other excited customers. Dee was agitated in awe of Kelley's "proven" talent, instantly suggested they should take his act out on the streets.

In the month of September 1583 Kelley as well as Dee were in Prague and jumped at the chance to promote their service to Emperor. In the past, Rudolf's advisers were likely to have many years of experience dealing with the crowds of fraudsters and quacks entering and exiting the castle gates and, as such they were skeptical of the duo's intentions. There were numerous attempts to inform the Emperor of their intentions and his advisors, only for each one to be denied. Rudolf welcomed the invitation to an audition. On the very same day Kelley was taken away to the tiny, unlit room in the basement, and then left to his own options at least that's what he thought. But in reality, Rudolf was observing his every move via a secret window within the wall. Kelley performed an incredible show, creating colorful smoke puffs and flashes of fire. As Rudolf "returned" just a couple of hours later, a shining Kelley dropped a large, chubby piece of gold into the hand of the emperor's bug-eyed hand.

The majority of people are of them agree that Kelley knew about the peephole for a long time and was simply able to make some gold he smuggled into his pocket before. This was among the oldest tricks of the book, yet the emperor was slain for it. Some naysayers also consider Enochian as the angelic language Kelley was said to be proficient within, completely fictional, and the two to be nothing less than professional con artist. However, when it comes down to whether Dee was a victim of shrewdness or an accomplice willing to the plot, the opinions differ in the middle. People who believe that Dee is innocent tend to take

Kelley's ability to deceive into account. Kelley is believed as being so convincing that Dee accepted to the angels' request that the exchange of wives.

Dee

Many chroniclers believe it could be this duo who wrote the Voynich Manuscript to secure the biggest payoff. There is a theory that, in addition to Jacobus, Kelley had been asked to unravel the manuscript. Like the man who has never experienced failure, he was successful in "deciphering" the text in a small portion the text by performing a magical seance. Kelley's fingers swung over the manuscript while the eyes of his crystal ball. Later, sent the messages via an Ouija-board of his own invention in the same way that Rudolf took in the entire experience.

In the event that Voynich Manuscript was , in actual fact a hoax, Kelley and Dee appear to match the timeline and profile to an extent. But, as it happens the case, should Rudolf had purchased the manuscript as early as the year 1600, Kelley could not have been the one who given it away since he died in 1597. It could also indicate that Dee who lived to 1608 had been tasked with delivering the book to the emperor. And the money could then be split between Kelley and his loved relatives.

However certain scholars believe that the Voynich Manuscript was not thought up out of greed however, but because of the necessity. Australian Author Stephen Skinner, a doctor from Australia. Stephen Skinner, for one, believes of the fact that it was composed by a frustrated Italian Jew who was looking for a secure method to share knowledge and cultural secrets at the time of the Christian persecution. This may also be the reason what makes the Voynich plants oscillate between reality and fantasy and the author believed that the plants could be easily identifiable to those who were interested, but being able to frighten when placed in incorrect hands. Skinner is a strong supporter of his theory by pointing out an additional distinctive aspect of the manuscript, naked nymphs residing in the green baths that Skinner has compared to ancient public baths that in the Jewish called"mikvah "mikvah." These mikvah, that are still in use within Orthodox Judaism, were designed to "purify" women who were going through menstrual cycle or birth. Skinner emphasized his argument by noting that there were no males in these baths and also he emphasized the nymphs' bulging bellies as well as the manuscript's absence of Catholic symbols. "There are no saints , nor crossesin the codex," stated Skinner. "Not even in the cosmic sections."

As plausible as Skinner's hypothesis may be, it's reasonable to bear in mind that even though Jews were subject to persecution during the most brutal years during the Inquisition, Jewish doctors were popular for their understanding of

Mediterranean botany. Because over half of the text was devoted to horticulture, the writer is most likely to be an Jewish doctor or at minimum, an herbalist. A lot of Jewish medical professionals also had a background in astrology, as a consult using the astrological signs was required to "determine the root of an illness as well as the treatment." With the idea of security and comforts that Jewish doctors enjoyed they were not the only ones who would have put up their lives for such an enticing venture. In the same vein of thought, other people might say that all it required was one courageous person to go beyond for the sake of ensuring that his legacy was forever secured.

Voynich's Unraveling

"There is another form of alchemy, functional and practical, that helps you make noble colors and noble metals as well as many other things more frequently by the art of making rather than as they are produced by the natural world." It is believed to be the work of Roger Bacon, 13th century English friar, philosopher and an alleged alchemist

A decade ago while aficionado of manuscripts Rene Zandbergen was browsing the Voynich archives, he discovered an important rediscovery that took the shape of specific document dating up to 17th century. This particular letter would reveal who the manuscript was destined to end ending up with following Jacobus de Tepenec's passing as An alchemist in Prague known as Georg Baresch.

As per the constant theme that appears to encompass most of the characters that have been linked to the manuscript, little information is available about Baresch. He was born in the Praguian countryside and, despite his family's financial struggles He enrolled in an Jesuit college, and later earned master's and bachelor's degrees in philosophy and liberal arts. In 1605's late April, Baresch came back to Prague after completing a different education in Rome.

In 1625, maybe earlier - he was a friend of Johannes Marcus Marci, a Bohemian scientist who was Rector from the University of Prague, and official doctor of his patron, the Holy Roman Emperor. The two shared a passion for all things philosophical and so the bond was instantly evident between them. 14 years after, Baresch journeyed to Rome for a business trip which is when the two came across Athansius Kircher who was who was a German Jesuit ecclesiastical scholar and polymath who was interested in cryptography as a side activity. Theywould also be friends for the rest of their lives, and would remain in contact through letters they exchanged regularly over the subsequent 25 years.

Marci

At the time of 1630 Baresch took over the Voynich Manuscript of Jacobus's estate however, the specifics of this transaction are not clear until today. Over the two decades Baresch was absorbed in the manuscript, attempting to crack the cipher from a variety of angles, but without success. Baresch was one of the authors who was working himself to close to tears for more than 20 years and had no evidence to prove it, was at a crossroads. In an impasse, he pleaded to his friend, Kircher, for aid. If anyone could understand the mysterious text, it was Kircher as he was an international celebrity after decoding the wall of Egyptian hieroglyphics that had been evading understanding for many years. The historians would later reveal the hieroglyphics decoding method of Kircher to be largely inaccurate However, at this point, Baresch had complete faith in his ability to decode the hieroglyphics.

Baresch wrote his first letter in the middle of February 1639. the letter revealed his frustration over his "impossible" manuscript in writing: "There is in my library, wasting my space, and a mystery in the form of the Sphinx." He outlined the illustrations and texts in the most professional manner to his ability however he was unable to do them justice. The only thing he could discern was that the book appeared to be a guide to botanicals or herbal reference guide, and he longed for an expert's opinion from his friend.

Kircher who was always up to take on a new challenge was intrigued by the concept of the manuscript right away. In his reply, Kircher attempted to coax Baresch into releasing the manuscript however Baresch who could see right through him, was sternly opposed to the idea. The note that Baresch wrote to Kircher telling him about the matter is believed to be laced with some sort of a sarcastic "patronizing" voice.

Baresch eventually decided to leave the manuscript to another old acquaintance, Marci, and upon Baresch's demise, Marci took possession of the manuscript. Marci was also equally competent for the job. Baresch recognized him as an eminent scientist and logic, who possessed determination and determination so unwavering even when he had been called as a blasphemer because he promoted "the study of embryogenesis and growth of human embryos." Marci would later refer to his friend's obsession with solving the mystery. "To solve it, he dedicated tirelessly," Marci wrote. "as it's apparent from his attempts his...and He gave up hope by the end of his life."

Marci was also unsuccessful in his attempt to discern the meaning of the confusing manuscript. In 1666, Marci took the codex and gave it to Kircher hoping that he would be able to have better luck. Unfortunately, the tracable story of the Voynich Manuscript ends at this point. There is no way to know whether Kircher ever recovered his poor reputation in the cryptography world, and it is generally believed that it was in the hands belonging to the Jesuits more than 300 years. In the midst of the Church's repression during the Society of Jesus, a period of tyranny and war that ran from 1750 to 1773, the text was believed to be transferred into the private library of Peter Beckx. Beckx was the superior General of the Order in the time of the incident, though aware of the potential inherently heretical content, was aware of the value of the manuscript, and decided to protect it from the hand of the Pope. His ex libris that was a custom bookplate, was discovered inscribed on the Voynich Manuscript after Voynich bought it in 1912.

Beckx

When Voynich removed the codex's cover to the very first time and uncovered a few yellowed slips of parchment, hidden within the manuscript fell into the air. The letter, similar to one that Zandbergen was able to stumble across nearly a century later it was written on the 19th of August 1666, written to Athanasius Kircher and was signed by Johannes Marcus Merci. This letter did not only give more information about the original owners of the manuscript and the author, but it also included the name of its supposed creator: Roger Bacon.

Voynich set out on a hunt for a needed decoding partner and discovered an ideal match with William Romaine Newbold, an professor in "intellectual as well as moral philosophy" in the University of Pennsylvania. Newbold was much more than an educated and well-educated professor, a name that was well-known in the realm of American academia. He was also a well-known pundit on the supernatural. He also wrote numerous works about the subject, including two pieces on the fabled "Great Chalice from

Antioch" that was a silver bowl with a stubby stem, decorated with gold-plated carvings, the identical Holy Grail that Christ had claimed to have used in The Last Supper.

Newbold

It didn't take long before Voynich convinced Newbold about Roger Bacon's contribution to the writing. The letter proved it and the two were ecstatic in identifying an extremely crucial elements in the Voynich puzzle the hand who wrote the letter. Roger Bacon, an English Franciscan friar and scientist, mathematician and philosopher of the 13th century was an intriguing persona. While he was a committed Christian, Bacon was an advocate for "natural magical practices." He was adamantly against magic incantations, spell-casting as well as"the "invocation of spirits" however, Bacon believed in the transformation of matter as well as other phenomena similar to that, which Bacon believed could only be accomplished by scientific and mathematical experimentation. He treated a lot of patients at his private clinics and many were nobility and awed them with his potent remedies that included an elixir which was believed to extend the lifespan of a person.

Due to Bacon's social standing and Franciscan connections, he had many documents and manuscripts to choose from and used them to broaden his perspectives. As time passed, his appearances at the library were becoming scarce. Instead, he was spending his time traveling around the world, meeting new cultures , and learning their customs and languages. When he wasn't traveling, he was working at his clinic working on some new experiment and continued to promote new remedies to the general public.

It was not very long until the Church discovered Bacon's business venture as a friar. Following a thorough reprimanding, and threat of exile, Bacon, much like the Italian Jew theory, was required to hide to avoid the scrutiny of the Clergy. At this point that Bacon was said to have wrote down his thoughts in hopes of immortalizing his "blasphemous" ideas with the most amazing cipher system that the entire world witnessed. Voynich would later praise Bacon when he wrote his essays, describing him as an "infinitely brilliant scholar, whoinferred from his writings the necessity of burying his most important secrets within the code."

The more they debated the subject and discussed the issue, and the deeper Voynich and Newbold became convinced regarding the authenticity of Bacon's manuscript, to the point that they were in a way, willing to put their money on the manuscript. They are believed to have pushed themselves to near-insanity during the following decade, with their attentions glued on the incomprehensible passages such a long time that they were into a watery red. Newbold in particular began to recognize clues that were scattered throughout the text, which grew as that he was immersed in the incomprehensible text. He discovered the "spiral Nebula" of the universe, and also references to fertilized eggs, human sperm and Fallopian tubes. For Newbold however his greatest surprise, what sealed his deal, and eventually caused his demise in the end was the bizarre and complicated case of "micro-letters." It was the method which he claimed to have discovered that he claimed to have been developed by Bacon is known as "anagrammed Micrographic Shorthand." Simply put Newbold claimed that the tiny "squiggles" appearing out of the characters of the manuscript's text had secret messages which could only be uncovered by means of anagrams. For the creation of these nano-sized squiggles, also known as "shorthand symbols" Newbold also claimed that Bacon invented the concept of a "usable compound microscope." In addition for mapping the stars that were found in the cosmological chapter of the manuscript which was a science that was not fully developed at the time, he constructed his personal model of a telescope in order to study the sky. Newbold was so obsessed with this specific element of the decryption of the manuscript, that as reported by The New Yorker, he lost his final years and deteriorating vision by using a magnifying lens that he carried in his hands.

Initially, Voynich and Newbold were recognized for their revolutionary research, and their theory was embraced by scholars from all backgrounds. "It will create the sensation of awe," Voynich predicted, before recounting the discussions he had with his coworker. "I I wish you could feel the excitement of the faces of his wife and professor. They danced and hugged each as well as me. They fell ill, depressed!"

The two partners put a new title on the codex called the Roger Bacon Cipher Manuscript - and then put it to the public, labeling the price at $100,000. It was then followed by an "Anglo-centric provenance" which was a document of ownership. In it, they claimed that it was not anyone else but John Dee who had sold the manuscript to the Emperor. The papers were abuzz in the wake of the discovery of the century or, according to some that it was the millennium, however, there was not one bit.

The whole thing came to a halt after historians started by examining and questioning the chronology of the source and disproved Newbold's assertions. They concluded that the symbols in shorthand are nothing but streaks and cracked paint that naturally occur as you get older. The gap Newbold was digging himself into was only widened after he acknowledged that his method of analysis were "inconsistent."

The first of Newbold's endorsers to criticize Newbold's views is John Matthews Manly, a "chief cryptologist" who was heavily utilized from The U.S. Army during the First World War. Manly released an apology retracting his endorsement and slammed Newbold for creating the mountain out of molehills, in which Manly explained that the "decipherments did not reveal secrets buried in the mind of Roger Bacon but the products of his intense passion as well as his ingenuous and knowledgeable unconscious." Twenty-first century American historian Lynn Thorndike threw more salt to the wounds with an obscene piece directed at Newbold that read "There isn't a single possibility in 50 years that Roger Bacon had any connection with the writing of the Voynich Manuscript." In September 1926, Newbold was killed suddenly of "acute stomach indigestion" and he would spend the rest of his life in a state of constant haunting by his mistakes and beset by the ridicule and snubs of his peers.

The first to took the initiative to debunk Newbold's theories, effectively destroying his credibility, and also tarnishing his legacy is William Friedman, another cryptographer for the U.S. Army. Friedman was praised as by the scholar David Kahn as the "world's greatest cryptologist" gained notoriety following his cracking of the Japanese Purple Cipher in World War II He is believed to have been the first to use computers to aid in decryption of text. The year 1925 was the time that Manly offered Friedman as well as his spouse, who was also a skilled decoder who was also a decoder, to take a stab in the Voynich Manuscript. They were certainly excited however, by the Second World War, they were forced to put the project back on the table until 1944. In 1944, they established Voynich Manuscript Study Group. Voynich Manuscript Study Group.

Friedman

Its members, made up of fellow colleagues and other highly regarded codebreakers, sat for the next forty years reminiscing about the photographs they received from Manly provided, however as with the others that came prior to them, they were unable to make a dent. Friedman as well as his spouse were able to take this in a more relaxed attitude, as they acknowledged their failure by writing an article from 1959 entitled "Acrostics, Anagrams, and Chaucer," published in the Philogical Quarterly. This article spoke of the displeasure of "annagramatic ciphers" contained a collection of jumbled wordswhich, was solved and revealed to be an actual anagram. In the event that Friedman passed away 11 years later the editor of Philogical Quarterly republished the article along with the long-awaited solution for the puzzle that summarized the team's final conclusion: "The Voynich Manuscript was the first attempt to create an artificial language, or universal language that was of the type a priori. - Friedman."

A few hours before dawn in March 1930, after an arduous and agonizing fight with cancer of the abdomen, Voynich was able to draw his final breaths and closed his eyes one final time. The widow of his husband Ethel who ultimately decided to give up the family's treasured possessions, and in 1961, the heirloom was given in 1961 to Hans Peter Kraus who was an eminent Viennese master of manuscripts from the medieval period. The price was of $24,500 and was given a share of the profits in the event that Kraus succeeded in securing an investor.

Kraus was determined negotiate the huge deal Voynich and Newbold long at for so many years, and so for a number of years Kraus enlisted the help of a group comprised of experts in restoration. In the beginning the he also banned other decoders from having physical entry to the book. Although the manuscript hadn't moved a centimeter when Voynich valued the manuscript with $100,000 in the first place, Kraus decided to go ahead and offered it up to the staggering amount of $160,000. Likely, there were few with such money to spare And even fewer would be willing to pay the size of the amount. In the end, hoping to lessen the pain, Kraus threw his weight in the ring and gave this codex Beinecke Library in Yale University, where it remains in the form of "MS-408."

Legacy

"This is an enticement and not trot. In reality, I cannot see any suitable way to unravel the very rare Voynich Manuscript. To me, the loss is very bleak." - - One of the anonymous contributions for Friedman's mind teaser

Today, the Voynich Manuscript is yet to be cracked, leaving the most renowned cryptographers of the world as well as lazy sleuths on the couch stunned and confused. Although many insist on the authenticity of the manuscript however, increasingly, more are beginning to call it a "hoax." A few claim that the true mysterious manuscript is as simple as the fact that it was on the tips of their noses throughout the whole time. Could be it that Voynich was the same person who brought the codex's cryptic nature in the eyes of the contemporary world, was in such a rush for fame that he knowingly created one of the biggest frauds that the world has ever witnessed?

Prior to the scandal's unraveling, Voynich, the cynical declarer, was in no way struggling to stay on the right track, however, halfway through his career, things was slowing. According to this theory, the moment Ethel was a renowned wordsmith, started to gain popularity within her field, her husband, who was jealous, began to think to come up with a revolutionary sales strategy to take the world to the forefront, and when it was impossible to locate the goldfish and decide to decide to take matters into himself. Perhaps the most intriguing thing is that in addition to his enviable history in the field of pharmaceuticals was also his unclean track record. For instance, the time he sold a fake version of Columbus Miniature. In addition witnesses claimed that the man was aware of the real source of the product.

The plethora of theories and speculations that remain connected to the manuscript will continue to rage on. Many have attempted to link the manuscript to the younger Leonardo da Vinci, and perhaps - as is usually when it comes to such things extraterrestrial oracles. But at the end the day there are historians who are not too jaded. Based on research conducted in recent years in addition to the cryptic manuscript's script follow "traditional language rules," its ink has been verified as authentic. Carbon dating has helped experts believe that the vellum is dated to 1420 at the earliest. Additionally, the majority of experts are of the opinion with the idea that "swallowtail castles" located in the Rosettes which are native of Northern Italy, hints at the author's nationality.

For now we can only wait until the right time comes to crack the code.

Chapter 5: Currier Language A And B

Captain Prescott Currier, a cryptographer was a cryptographer who looked at the Voynich several years ago and made some insightful observations on the manuscript. Particularly, Currier noticed that the handwriting was different between Folios, as well as other ones. And Currier also observed (based on the number of glyphs) it was possible to distinguish two "languages" that were being used:

"When I first started looking through the text, I was thinking about the initial (roughly) fifty pages comprising that section of herbal. The first twenty-five folios within this section of the book are clearly with one hand, and the other is a "language," which I dubbed "'A." (It could have been named anything , it was simply the first one I could think of.) The next twenty-five or so folios are written in two hands and are clearly the work of at most two distinct men. Additionally the text in this second section of the section on herbs (that means the following twenty-five of the thirty folios) is written in two languages as well as each "language" is written by its individual hand. This implies that, despite being two authors for the second section of the section on herbs each wrote in their own "language. It's true that I'm stretching my point somewhat, but I'm aware. My use of the word "language" is a good idea, but it doesn't carry the same meaning that it does in normal usage. However, it's an acceptable word and I can see no reason to not continue employing the word." -Currier Currier

To clarify To be clear, the thing Currier discovered was that one of the words frequency found in the initial twenty-five herb pages are distinct from the word frequencies of the twenty-fiveth folio. It's quite remarkable. In actual fact, the entire manuscript could be divided roughly into two sets of folios. These are that which were written "Language A" as well as the ones that are written using "Language B". Of course, because we do not know what the terms actually mean, it is not possible to declare that the language is different, only that the frequency of words are different.

For instance the ten most popular words found in the Language A herbal folios are written as daiin, chol the chor, s, the CThy, Shol, Sho, dar, dy, and chy. While in Language B, the ten most used terms in the herbal folios include aiin or daiin, chedy ar, dar shedy, qokedy and chckhy. It is possible to observe that the only word which is common on each list is daiin. It turns out that there are some words that are used often in Language A however they are not used as often are they found on Language B. For instance, cThy appears more than 60 times within the Language A folios, but only once in the Language B folios. In contrast, 4okain is found around 160 times in Language B folios, but only one time in the A folio (and maybe that one folio was incorrectly assigned with Language A)!

What could be the possible explanations for these strange changes? A theory suggests that, as it was the case that the document was composed in the first place, the code or transcription changed slowly or as the scribes got more proficient in writing it. One theory states that settings of the cipher were changed those folios that were being written and when B folios were being written , possibly using an cipher wheel or another mechanism that was used to facilitate the enciphering process was set to the other. Another theory is that Language variations result from different phonetic transcriptions of the natural spoken language that was being translated: one person who transcribed the sound heard it differently than the other or there were a variety of people who were transcribed speech and each with a different accent or intonations.

The Gallows Glyphs

The glyphs of the Voynich words are mixed with standard medieval script characters and strange glyphs that look similar to this: t k and p. There is no plausible explanation for what the glyphs that are referred to as "Gallows" symbols, mean. Also, no one has explained the reason why gallows glyphs can be "benched" (see 3 in Figure 3.) and look like in the form of F T K. It is interesting to note that when Gallows are benched they are usually layered with symbols that look similar to C H, so that the glyphs appear like this, such as the glyph CPH. The first word of each folio, as well as in every paragraph, is usually an glyph of the gallows, but they can also appear within the middle of words. Another thing to note is that Gallows glyphs are almost never seen as the final glyph of the word.

On different folios, the initial gallows glyph appears heavily embellished. The examples are illustrated in Figure 4.

Certain researchers have proposed that the gallows' glyphs are capital letters since they are often found at the beginning of the word that appears on an article, as is noted. Embellishments on letters that begin with initial letters are commonplace in medieval manuscripts, consequently, what we see on the gallows give credence to the idea of capital letters. For the gallows with benches There are theories that they're phonetic variations of the glyphs that are not benched.

Whatever the glyphs in the gallows are meant to mean and represent, the locations they appear in on each folio exhibit peculiar characteristics. Figure 5 illustrates one of the folios found in the so-called "Recipes" section near the very end of the manuscript:

The diagram shown in Figure 6 is derived from a transcription of the f112r It's an pixel map of the position of the glyphs f.gallows (red pixels) and the p Gallows (blue pixels) and the rest of the symbols (black pixels) on the Folio.

The most obvious thing by the illustration is the p symbols (blue) prefer to be located at the beginning of lines. In the case of the two f symbols (red) The one is the first character on the folio right at the start of the first line while the second appears mid-way across the folio, but not near the beginning of a line. Maybe the affinity that the gallows glyphs share with the folio's start and line is merely evidence that every "recipe" that appears on the page starts with an uppercase letter? Or is it an signal it was positioned on the folio according an unidentified scheme or arrangement?

The Fouro Glyph(s)

Through the manuscript's text we find numerous words that begin with the glyph combination 4o. However, it is rare to see the pair in the middle or at the end of the word. In fact, the 4 glyph is almost never seen alone without the or. Some have believed the meaning that the word 4o stands for an alphabetic pair which are often unbreakable. In English this couple is "qu" which means that words such as the word qokol could translate the word "queen" for instance "queen" when the language of the plaintext is English. There is speculation that 4o could be one of the many prefixes or suffixes being encoded, or maybe an individual glyph. If you look in details at the folios in which it is found, it is evident from strokes of the pen or quill in that it is written an individual glyph in many instances. But, on the other hand writing a "qu" will often appear like it was written as one glyph.

daiin daiin daiin

Here's one of the most interesting aspects that the passage. There are several instances where we can encounter this similar Voynich word repeated three times or even three times. A good example can be seen in Figure 7, where the word daiin appears repeatedly.

In this instance, a an examination of the final symbols n shows that they are slightly different The top loops have a different angle and the inking suggests maybe they were added later. However, are these differences really significant?

Another example is in Figure 8, where the process of chol repeats three times.

It is a challenging aspect to understand for the majority of theories about ciphers. There are some contrived instances of this from English in which the exact word is used several times such as: "All the faith he previously had did not have any influence on the course that he experienced in the course of his existence." (There are many more examples like this at https://en.wikipedia.org/wiki/List_of_lin guistic_example_sentences.) What is the reason such concoctions occur in the text of an early medieval period? Maybe it is Plainchant that is, the repetitive repetition of same phrases and words? But If it's plainchant, why don't we not notice other parts of the Voynich text that is repeated in the same manner?

It is worth noting that the examples given for repeated usages of the Voynich word daiin, and extremely common words in the manuscript. They aren't uncommon words.

Another explanation for the reason why word repetitions are that they're byproducts of the enciphering process or unexpected redundancies or mistakes, in the code.

Or Or R

In addition to repetitions of words There are many fascinating visual examples of glyphs being repeated over several words. A good example can be seen in f15v in Figure 9 , where the glyph pair repeats four times within the row.

This particular aspect that is present in this text difficult to explain, unless the characters represent numbers in some manner (see The Theory of Numbers below).

Sequences of Differently Spelled Words

Many words differ only by one or two letters, and a few words with a small spelling variations often appear in order. A f66r example is depicted in Figure 10.

This is the text line that reads: qokeeody qokeody the qokar sheky qokeeody word okedy where the first word is different from the second one symbol, the third is the same as the second word, the fourth word is similar prefix to the other three words, as well as the final word, which is repetition of the previous. It's hard to come up with an other language with these kinds of spelling patterns in words when it's written.

One way to quantify the significance of this feature is to examine the"edit distance" or "edit distance" between two words. This is the amount of edits to a single character needed for transforming one word to another. For instance an edit distance of terms "hid" or "had" is one because only one character needs to be changedfrom "i" in the sentence to "a". Natural language prose generally is characterized by a long average edit distance. This can be seen simply by looking at each sentence of this sentence for instance and then mentally adding the editing needed to transform every word into its succeeding. But, if the words are ordered alphabetically, the editing distance decreases. Are we reading in the text of the file f66r? Do these Voynich words been recorded in a certain sequence?

The intriguing idea was suggested by the researcher Philip Neal, who gave the following directions: 1.) Divide an unstructured text into lines, 2.) sort the text on each line alphabetically 3) Sort the words' letters to alphabetical sequence. Philip provides the following illustration:

One thing led to the next the other night

Another last night led one to do that

aehnort alst del ghint eno ot ghint ghint

In this example in the example, we can see how 2 words "thing" come together and also how certain letters, such as "t" generally be placed in the middle of words. These are strong reminiscences of patterns we've observed in the Manuscript's texts.

The Month Names

Folios 70-73 The folios 70 through 73, also known as the Zodiac Folios, display twelve circular charts. Some are with fold-outs. The center on each chart is tiny illustrations of various creatures, objects and peoplethat are associated to those of the Zodiac signs. Around the circles are several female figures, most of them naked, the quantity of which differs between charts.

The folios are usually believed to represent the months of the year as well as signs of the Zodiac The images could represent the levels of each sign. In fact, on each of the central illustrations is a month's name, written in plain text. The writings, in contrast to the other text on the folio, appear to be written later, using another hand, once the manuscript had been completed. The style of handwriting used in the month's names is like those of "Michiton Oladabas" writing style on f116v which we'll look at later.

As you can see in the chart below the spelling of names of the months is fascinating and so is the connection between those of the Zodiac signs. (January as well as February appear to be not included from the Manuscript, nearly probably due to the existence of the missing folio, F74 which was lost.)

What is the language that these month names were written in? Perhaps , if we could find the language, we could determine what language the remainder of the manuscript was enciphered from? It could also be the language of another hand, perhaps someone who is trying to understand the drawings. Based on http://www.omniglot.com/language/tim e/months.htm the language Occitan (from a region in Spain) appears to be a decent (but underwhelming) match. (Some researchers would prefer the match to medieval Northern French.) It is worth noting that the Occitan names are in the table below, along with the the number of figures in the puzzle (we'll investigate that puzzle in the next) and the Zodiac signs that seem to match the drawings.

Table 1 Names of the Month as well as Figure Counts and Zodiac signs on the Folios of 70 to 73

Nomination Numbers for Folio Months of Figures Zodiac Sign English/Occitan

F70v2 mars (marc?) 29 March/marc Pisces

F70v1 aberil 15 April/abril Aries (Dark)

f71r aberil 15 April/abril Aries (Light)

f71v may 15 May/mai Taurus (Light)

f72r1 may 15 May/mai Taurus (Dark)

f72r2 jong (?) 30 June/Junh Gemini

f72r3 jollet (?) 30 July/julhet Cancer

f72v3 augst 30 August/agost Leo

F72v2 September (?) 30 September/setembre Virgo

f72v1 octebre 30 October/octobre Libra

f73r novebre 30 November/novembre Scorpio

f73v decebre 30 December/decembre Sagittarius

In the above summary In the summary above, April and May are presented with two diagrams. Why is that? Let's examine the two May sketches side by side:

The two roundels for May.

The figures in every diagram count 15 which is 10 on the outer ring and five in the middle, making the total of 30. Since May has 31 days, the numbers cannot represent days of the month.

There is a possibility that these 30 divisions aren't actually days, but rather degrees. The degree corresponds to a particular stone (like diamond, sapphire and others) and was believed to possess supernatural power. This Lapidary of Alfonso X "The Learned" is a thirteenth-century text that is dedicated to gemstones that was written by hand in Castillian (old Spanish), and is a translation from an more ancient Arabic document. Illustrations of the Lapidary is below.

Taurus is in the Alfonso X Lapidary

This lapidary folio depicts Taurus. It is evident that there are characters of animals, people and even animals depicted within every one of these 30 segments and in the center, there is a bull identified by the cluster of star constellations. The text accompanying the Lapidary provides the stones that are connected to every 30 degree and how they are connected to the stars of Taurus. Taurus. Perhaps the Zodiac pages from the Voynich Manuscript are discussing the characteristics of stones and that the pictures of stars indicate the stars in the constellations?

The Cipher Key and Picnic Table Glyph

In scouring through the manuscript's folios numerous researchers have discovered clues that could be cipher keys that are in the form letters or numbers. These sequences are prevalent on f49v and f57v as well as the f66r, f75v, and f76r and are illustrated on Figure 12, and Figure 13.

In f69r we find a second sequence, this time inside circles, located in the middle of this diagram. O l s em y

The circular diagram in the f57v (Figure 14 in the next) is particularly interesting because it's different from other circular diagrams within the manuscript that typically show the month or the stars. Contrary to this, f57v features four human figures within the central roundel and an outer set of circular rings that contain letters and symbols.

The beginning point of the sequences of text/glyphs that are found in the rings is around 10 hour. When looking at the ring one through from the outside the glyphs appear placed into four similar set of 17. Each set of 17 appears like this:

o l d r v x k m f (c) t r a O y l !

Table 3: The sequence of 17 Glyphs on f57v

What are these 17 glyphs representing? A few of these glyphs are extremely uncommon in the manuscript, like the"picnic table" or "picnic table" symbol in position six: x , and the "reclining figure" glyph at the position of 10: (c). It is possible that the 17 glyphs represent 22 letters of the classic Latin alphabet, but with vowels (A,E,I,O,U) taken out, i.e. BCDFGHLMNPQRSTXYZ. Perhaps the picnic table symbol is "Z" due to its popularity? Another interesting aspect in the series is that glyph V is located in the fifth position. This is a glyph that appears to be an upside-down V. This is the Roman numeral for 5.

Another possibility, as suggested by researchers Nick Pelling, is that the sequence may actually be 18 glyphs in length - with some of them from Table 3 is a combination of two glyphs that are joined: O . This gives 72 glyphs within the rings i.e. each glyph is 5 degrees, which is 360 total.

Key Sequence Summary

The table below summarizes the sequences of events observed:

Folio Key Sequence

49v o r y e ~

57v o l d r v x k m f @ t r a O y l !

66r y o s sh y d o r f * x air d sh y f f y o d r f c r x t o * l r t o x p d

69r d o l s em y

75v s l l o r

76r s d q s o l k r s

As with of the information in the Manuscript it is the sequences that turn out to not be particularly interesting. In essence, every sequence is unique making their interpretation difficult. We can even speculate that the the glyphs on f49v that are which are numbered from 1 to 5 and corresponding to the numbers?

Coda of Urbino (1440)

Researchers seeking to determine the source of the glyphs found in the Manuscript are naturally interested in studying the ciphers that were invented in the medieval period. There are a variety to pick from. A good instance (noted by the d'Imperio) could be one called the "Code of Urbino" which dates from 1440 and detailed in Figure 15.

Certain of the glyphs utilized in this cipher are like Voynich Manuscript glyphs. For instance, 4o is for QUO, an x to represent and p for. Additionally, I find it interesting to note that the cipher employs nulls: These are glyphs that, when seen in the text of the cipher, represent no letters in any way - they're simply included to make deciphering more difficult. The other impact they may create is to alter apparent distribution of word lengths. If there are a lot of nulls, the length of plaintext words deciphered are generally shorter than the words in the cipher. Nulls could be the reason we have only a few single glyph words found in this Voynich Manuscript. However it is highly unlikely that a cipher similar to the one used in the Urbino instance will be employed in the Manuscript because it is not the reason for some aspects we've seen, such as the repetition of words and groups of glyphs. It is more likely the possibility that an Urbino-like cipher may have been employed in conjunction with an other method of processing the plaintext. For instance, an earlier alphabetical kind of plaintext words that were to be written or an arrangement on the folio in accordance with the unspecified prescription, then encryption using an Urbino encryption technique, could account to the pattern we have observed.

Chapter 6: The Armadillo

There are a variety of animals represented in the drawings of the Manuscript. Certain of their names have been the subject of debate, such as for instance the "armadillo" depicted in the f80v, which is shown on Figure 22. Are these really armadillo, a species that was first discovered from South America, a location which is not in line with the style of other illustrations in the manuscript, such as castles or actually pangolin (scaly antiater) or a pangolin (scaly anteater) from Asia or Africa?

Maybe it's not an armadillo nor a pangolin and is instead an imagined creature similar to the dragon depicted in f25v and illustrated on Figure 23?

The Spread Eagle

The spread eagle represents an interpretation for the root of the plant that is f46v as seen in figure 24. What ever it represents it's a bit fanciful and unreal as a root of a plant. Despite that, and as mentioned earlier the drawing of root systems in this extravagant style was common in the medieval herbals of alchemical chemistry. So, as Voynich Manuscript puzzles go it's a long way to the bottom of the league table!

Jars Jars

The section that is part of the Voynich Manuscript referred to by the name of "pharmaceutical section" comprises a number of smaller sketches of plain appearance plants, all captioned, and set in vibrant containers. They are similar to traditional containers used to store herb and ointments, also known as"apothecary" jars or "albarellos". Most jars come with labels that are written on them and this adds to the idea that the author of the article also did the sketches. A sample of the jars can be seen on Figure 25.

However, are they really images of apothecary jars? Could they be something different? Research suggests that, instead of containers, the drawings show the use of microscopes, candlesticks salt cellars, needle-cases and Egyptian perfume bottles. While the most likely explanation is that they're the apothecary jars due to the similarity to illustrations of herbs as well as roots, the most puzzling aspect is that some jars have pilasters (seen in the illustration from F88r1) or even feet (seen in the illustration from the f89r1) These are features not common to albarellos from the past and Jars.

The Castles in the Rosettes

"Rosettes "Rosettes" refers to the name that is given to a fold-out part from the Voynich Manuscript which is comprised of nine folios. It is illustrated on Figure. It is believed to be a kind of map that shows nine circular areas linked. The meaning of what these areas represent is purely speculation. No one has yet come with a convincing explanation of what they mean and the reason why they're laid out in this way. Certain aspects seem to suggest that they are maps. One of them is the appearance of castles, or the tiniest of details.

The most striking castle is illustrated in figure 27. The most striking aspect of the castle is the design of the battlements, square uprights, also known as "merlons" that have the notch in the shape of a V. The design is referred to as the swallowtail or Ghibelline or the merlon. Italian stonemasons began to create these designs in the 1300s. We are aware that the vellum from the Voynich Manuscript was carbon-dated as early as the 1400s, the representation of swallowtail merlons seems to be in line with the fact that it was an Italian castle, even though it isn't able to pin the area down with certainty.

The other characteristics of the castle are not exceptional An arcaded gateway with two square keep and a conical-shaped roofed tower. Let's look at additional castles that are part of the Rosettes Check out the figure 28.

The castle shown in the top drawing is comprised of four towers. Two have conical roofs one with an azure flat roof and another that has a roof decorated by two staffs. Finding online images of, or medieval manuscripts with drawings ofsimilar castles is an excellent opportunity to spend a few hours. A possible match could be located in the archives online from Frankfurt University, from a 1460 document written by Conradus Keyser. It is believed to contain strategies and methods of fighting castles. It can be seen in Figure 29. In the image, four people are seen hiding under two covers that appear to be like giant thimbles. The fifth person is believed to be engaged in the process of destroying an of the castle's towers. It is evident the similarities to the castle in this drawing as well as the one shown in the drawing on top of Figure 28.

The diagram that is shown in figure 28 different, as it appears to show one tower. Some have suggested it's "in an abyss" due to the line shading that surrounds the tower.

The drawings of castles and towers from the Rosettes are strikingly similar to the look of a castle that exists in the present: Castle Runkelstein in Northern Italy. Furthermore, Castle Runkelstein contains several medieval frescos dating back to the 1300s and later, that include paintings that remind us of drawings found in the Voynich Manuscript. For instance, one fresco depicts an edifice (shown on Figure 30) with the roof and towers in similar style to the one we've just seen.

The battlements of the swallowtail merlon can be clearly seen when we look at the fresco of Figure 30 and we can discern them in the modern photo of the castle shown in Figure 31. It's important to note that the style of this castle differs from the way it been in the medieval period For instance, one of the castle's towers was accidentally blow up during the 1500s. It is important to note that the design of the faces of the three people standing in front of the castle shown in figure 30 are like the faces found in the manuscript.

Are the castles on the Rosettes real or fictitious? If they're real castles, are those castles still exist? If yes, then their location will provide a clear indication of where the person who wrote the manuscript was and where he took his or her inspiration.

"The Naked Ladies and Pipes

The part that is part of the Voynich Manuscript, whose contents are possibly the most puzzlesome is known as the Balneological Folios. These folios show several female figures, with various postures, and an interconnected system of tubs platforms, baths and baths. The liquids flowing are color green and blue, while the pipes appear as if they are gushing steam or drops of water. A typical illustration can be seen in Figure 32. Here we can see a woman who is seen altering a set pipe and nozzles pointed toward her. One nozzle spraying liquid. It is obvious that the folios refer to an spa or bathing facility.

Researchers have conducted extensive searches through a variety of medieval manuscripts (and unlike the illustrations in the Herbal or Zodiac folios which have a lot of similarities with other documents) however, no convincingly identical drawings of pipes interconnected or baths, nozzles, or nozzles are found in any other works. The nature of females being the only gender shown in the folios leads to conclusion that the topic of the balneological folios are treatment and remedies for women. In that regard certain researchers have observed significant similarities between the design of baths and pipes in the folios, e.g. the fallopian tubes and Ovaries (f77v) as well as the heart (f77r).

The Archer

This illustration from f73v which is related with that of the zodiac sign Sagittarius is a depiction of an image of a crossbow as shown in Figure 33. It is one of the few illustrations found in the manuscript that are non-controversial. There is no debate about the details depicted. It has been a thorough investigation of the identity of the weapon, as well as of the date of the clothing worn by the man and headgear, in particular.

The crossbow's design in f73v has been examined and compared with the evolution of the weapon over the ages and across various regions. The most closely matched designs date back in the late late1400s and can be located throughout Central European German, and North Italian manuscripts. This is in fact, very compatible with the carbon-dated date to the Voynich Manuscript from 1440. these dates are also consistent with the headgear that the archer was wearing.

The Pleiades

A folio which includes circular diagrams with stars is the f68r3. The segment of the diagram has a small star cluster with seven lights that is similar to that of the Pleiades stars cluster provided you know some about astronomy. Figure 34 depicts the star cluster that is labeled onlyy and is drawn in close proximity to the larger star, which bears the designation dceolday .

If the cluster of seven stars is in fact the Pleiades and the next star must be the Aldebaran. We could have two word cribs within the cipher. A lot of students have attempted to make use of this crib to gain some insight into an understanding from the text, however none of them have been even significantly successful.

If you look closer do those stars actually supposed to be Aldebaran and the Pleiades as well as Aldebaran? The actual form of the galaxy as seen by the naked eye (on an evening with clear skies!) is different, and the location of Aldabaran's position is from. Figure 35 illustrates what it appears to be.

What is the significance behind the mysterious curved line that runs across the entire cluster until what is the significance of Sun in the center of this diagram?

The Clock

There's a tiny portion of the Rosettes folded out folios, with an illustration that has been compared to a clock's face check out the figure 36. The identification first sparked fascination from a manuscript date perspective that clocks with hands were developed in the late medieval period.

But a closer examination of the drawing dispels the idea that it's an actual clock. The central point for the hands isn't located in the centre of the circular area, due to instance and it is also apparent that the "hands" are all identical in length - not a great way to tell the time! Actually, does this appear much more like an image similar to one of the symbols of alchemy for Gold that is shown in figure 37?

Jointed Faces and Maps with T/O

The T/O Map (Orbis Terrarum) is a form of world map from the medieval period which splits a circle into three pieces by using three T. One early illustration is in Figure 38. Here, the three regions of the globe are identified as Asia, Africa and Europa.

The Voynich Manuscript has several drawings that appear like T/O Maps.

Incredibly, the drawings also contain words that could be a hint into the code.

The first illustration can be found in the T/O Map on folio 68v3 which is illustrated on Figure 31. Two quadrants are adorned with the words otodol as well as opcholdg which could be referring to Europe/Jafeth and Africa/Cham and Europa/Jafeth, respectively (we have to think about rotating the map 180 degrees to ensure that it is in line with that of the Isidore map). The semicircle is populated with the words"only ykeol darol daly solaiin Olekeey Dy Ykeol Ctheepchy and how it corresponds to Asia/Sem has been a challenge Perhaps it's an explanation of Asia?

Another T/O Map is also found inside the Rosettes. Quality of Beinecke scan is not great on this folio, as shown in Figure 32. However, the Voynich words appear to be Okas (Africa) Opac9 (Europa) Osal (Asia).

The Figure 32 Map of T/O from the Rosettes

However, these circular diagrams we've examined might not be as they appear as they are similar to other aspects that are in the document. Maybe they're not T/O maps in any way. An indication that they might not be T/O maps is evident in f67v that shows the faces of four different sets, with one in every edge of the book (Figure 33). The left-hand corner set depicts four faces within the "T/O Map" style drawing, however, faces in the face-drawings look different from T/O Maps. Furthermore the term T/O Map by definition is meant to depict the three regions, and not just four regions, as long as one assumes the fact that on these Map each region is identified with faces, not words.

In the next part, we will find another instance in that T/O Map shape appearing in the Manuscript even though it's invisible from sight.

Scratches

In a few Folios (shown in figure 34) If you look closely, you can see what on first glance are marks on the velvet. If we look closer, these scratches reveal themselves to have been written. In f86v3, the writing is in the form of a T/O Map, similar to those described in the earlier section.

The letters are difficult to discern and they're not exactly like the glyphs found in the manuscript's text. Researchers have speculated that what we see may be the handwriting of an earlier owners of this book however, why they could write their name so badly and in a faint manner in one of the folios isn't understood. Another possibility is that they marks were that the scribe made while working with a new pen and testing it before taking the plunge to write the text. In this scenario it is probable that the signature shown is the signature of the scribe.

Bad Porridge

On the left side of folio 66r you will see an elderly woman lying on her stomach. To her right is what seems to be a pot as well as two circular items speckled with speckles possibly food or medication. The drawing can be seen on Figure 35.

The figure that is reclined as well as her pots and medications There are four plaintext words which are "y", "den", "mus" and "del" (although the meanings differ). When you input these words to Google Translate, it detects that the language used in plaintext is Spanish and has a translation to English: "and give mus". "Mus" is an Spanish games of cards, however it was invented in the 17th century, and this interpretation is not satisfactory. It's also not useful as a way to instruct the disabled to play a game! This indicates that we've misunderstood the words. According to some researchers, these words mean "der mu del" which is an older German to mean "der Mussteil", meaning "the widow's part" . Other researchers have proposed the words could be "den mus"mel" which is similar to "the porridge flour" in German and Dutch. Maybe the lady has consumed some toxic porridge that was made from poor quality flour? It could be another instance where something is written in the Manuscript which at first seems to be straightforward and easy to understand turns out to be obscure and difficult to determine.

Miscellaneous Curiosities

There are many illustrations in the Manuscript that could entice the shrewd reader to take a second glance. Some examples are presented in the following figures.

A note about the gap in the paper of f34v indicates that it seems to have been made intentionally or perhaps through rubbing and it isn't a genuine gap in the paper. One possibility suggests that Voynich Manuscript was of a long-lost original. When copying f34 the scribe was at attempt to recreate a hole that was visible in the original page.

the Puzzle the Folio The Ordering

The Folios that comprise the Voynich Manuscript are encased in covers that aren't originally designed: they were later added, probably after the initial covers failed, and were removed, or were discarded. Additionally, some folios of the manuscript's original are missing, as previously mentioned and some seem to be missing from the order they were originally.

For instance, f78v illustrates women in the bath with green water that has an entry pipe or stream from the left side, and two pipes leaving from the bottom of the bath. See Figure 43, which shows the front folio of the f79r.

If we instead place the folio f81r alongside f79r It seems to work better. Both folios have identical baths, and the pipes connect on the outside that separates the two.

This indicates that in the first binding, folio 81 was the first page, and not folio 80. It was then followed by the folio the 79.

Maybe the binding broke at some point and that book fell down to the ground with its covers destroyed beyond repair, the fragments scattered throughout? Perhaps the owner rebuilt them in a nearly right order, before putting on new covers? The questions are what was the initial folio's layout and what was the content of those missing pages?

Chapter 7: First Folio

You'll notice the poor condition of the vellum was a victim of finger and thumb rubbings and scratched over the decades of usage and also damaged by bookworms and damp, among other destructive factors. The words written on the vellum are slightly faded and smudged even with a few minor changes made to the image shown in the figure. It is evident that the green leaves in that drawing located on the reverse part of the page appear through the thin velvet.

Many researchers believe that the first folio serves as an opening to the text and contains short descriptions of the subjects discussed. The three intricate red letter glyphs on this page are intriguing They don't look exactly like the glyphs found elsewhere in the manuscript or are recognized characters from medieval literature, as per researchers (although the first one is similar to topic markers or paragraphs discovered within Spanish documents). It's possible they're obscure symbols of alchemy.

The Text

To comprehend how the Voynich Manuscript is all about it is essential to be able to comprehend it. The text has been researched as possibly a cipher, code or the transcription of natural language. Researchers are comprised of highly educated and knowledgeable experts in linguistics, cryptographers and linguistics in the study of ancient manuscripts. They together with a number of amateurs, have been unable to provide an explanation that is convincing about how the manuscript was written but not a single word has been decoded to the delight to more than handful of people, possibly deluded!

First line on the f17r

The text displayed above is the first line in Folio 17r. A few of the letters are easily identifiable such as "8", "9", "o", "a" as well as an alphabet that looks similar to the letter "2". The other letters are more mysterious and are more obscure, like the initial letter of the first word, which is reminiscent of the shape of a flagpole. The second letter is two "c"s joined with an squiggle over. The word position of some letters are obvious: "9" mostly appears at the beginning or the in the middle of a phrase, and it isn't at the center.

In the following sections, we will examine the appearance and the properties of Voynich words as well as their glyphs that compose them, the obvious rules that govern the way they appear in the labels on the illustrations, as well as comment on how certain aspects continue to confuse attempts at decoding the manuscript.

Entropy

One of the most important questions we must ask ourselves concerning the text is Does it have a meaning? One way to determine whether the text contains details is to look at its Entropy. Shannon Entropy Shannon Entropy of a string of text measures the amount of information that is contained within the text. For text that is totally random i.e. that every character's look is equally likely as any other character, the amount of entropy (which is referred to in the sense of "disorder") will be extremely. Contrarily when a text is a lengthy sequence of similar characters is the one with the lowest entropy. It contains the smallest amounts of details. Text that falls somewhere between contains either more or less data. While we can't understand the Voynich Manuscript's language but we can gauge its the entropy. If the entropy is very high then the text could appear to be random gibberish. If it's lower the text is likely to contain details, since it's highly ordered.

Mathematically mathematically, Shannon Entropy can be described mathematically. Shannon Entropy is defined as:

To determine the Entropy We first determine probabilities (called Probi in the equation above) of every glyph we find in the Manuscript. It is simply the number of times the glyph appears multiplied by N, which is the total number of letter appearances. Once we know the Probi on each of the glyphs we can determine the Entropy by going through every glyph they appear throughout the folios and then sum the probability for each one times its logarithm.

Let's take a look at some of the results of using the Entropy for different texts:

Word Source Text Entropy

None Random Gibberish 6.0

Medieval Italian Dante 1320 4.2

English Thomas Hardy 1874 4.2

German Cookbook 1553 4.1

Spanish Medina 1543 4.1

Latin Cantus Planus 4.0

French Text since 1367 4.0

Voynich Voynich Manuscript 3.7

"Random Gibberish" in the table "Random gibberish" that appears in this table, is an artificially created text that has letters selected randomly in the alphabet. Other results result by analyzing a variety of texts in various languages, along with the findings on Voynich Manuscript. Voynich Manuscript.

The results are obvious The results are clear: according to this test, the manuscript's text is well-organized and distinct from random gibberish. It is clear that there is some meaning in the text.

Certain researchers prefer using an "second second" Entropy as a measure that is comparable as Shannon's Shannon Entropy, except it rather shows the likelihood of finding a glyph or letter in relation to the previous one. Second order Entropy also shows a low value in the case of the Manuscript.

The Voynich result shown in the above table is discovered by using the EVA transliteration of the manuscript's texts into computer-readable characters. The transcription was done by Takeshi Takahashi. The transcription of the Voynich text isn't an easy task, as the exact alphabet used in the text isn't known. Therefore, it is necessary to decide what characters in the text are to be translated as a single letter of the alphabet, or as multiple characters joined. For instance the glyph ce is a single character or is it a combination of two characters, c or e? The type of transcription you choose will impact the Entropy measure in a certain degree.

The Labels

Along the edges of many of the drawings are written words It's likely that these are captions or labels. One peculiar aspect of these labels is that they have the word(s) that appear on the label are almost never seen in any other text elsewhere on the same leaflet. This is a bit surprising. If you're writing about plants and have a page dedicated to the dangerous nightshade. It would have a picture of the plant and likely write the name "Deadly Nightshade" on it. When you describe the plant,, you'd likely use the terms "deadly" along with "nightshade" at the very least. However it's not the case on the Voynich Manuscript it is evident that the majority of the words used on labels on a specific folio don't show up in the texts on the folio, even though they are within the Manuscript.

It is possible that, as suggested by this anomaly that the drawings on the folio aren't in any way connected with the text printed on the folio.

Another intriguing aspect of the labels is how the exact label word can be found on totally different illustrations. For instance, the word Otol89 appears alongside objects on five different folios, however, there is no apparent connection with the items it's labeling as seen in Figure 2 where the five labels that appear are highlighted with red bars. There are also counter-cases like the label otal89 that appears on the folios 99r, 88r and 101v2 beside plants that could be the identical root. As an illustration of a label that may identify an identical object certain pages, but is an entirely different object on other the label Otal9. It appears on folios 84r 99v, 88r, and 84r: It labels a root on 99v and 88r, but is part of the ladies tub piping system on the 84r.

Chapter 8: The Drawings

The Plants

When first viewed, we begin to go through it the Voynich Manuscript is quite like a medieval herbal (albeit with odd writing) The first dozen folios contain plants or plants with strangely shaped roots. A lot of researchers fail to see beyond the similarities and are quickly convinced it's a plant and the problem is to recognize the plants. The result is frustration, as each plant or herb becomes more difficult to recognize than what it appears to be maybe because we're familiar with beautiful images of plants? Let's look at just two examples.

The Sunflower

The plant that is in Figure 19 was identified by the botanist (O'Neill) from the 40s, as an New World Sunflower, despite the fact that it appears unlike an actual Sunflower to the casual observer. The discovery sparked fascination at the time considering that Sunflowers might only have been identified by an European writer following Columbus traveled to America in 1493.

If Sunflowers were mentioned The Voynich Manuscript, some assume that the reference refers to the plant that is depicted in Figure 20 on the left, on f33v.

It's more like Sunflowers despite the blue flowers on the flower and the bizarre root balls. Because medieval Alchemical Herbals are filled with images of bizarre roots and the blue petals could be artistic license, can this really be Sunflowers after all?

Letters in Plants

A number of sketches in the manuscript seem to be colored after drawing the outline in the ink. Sometimes, tiny letters can be seen through the paint or in the areas that are not colored in the drawings. Two examples can be seen in Figure 21. The uppermost part of the root displays the letters "r or t" while in the center of leaf on the bottom has a small "b".

Could this mean that the plant on the left was destined to be dyed in red ("rot" to German) in German, and that the space between the leaves to be blue, blau or bleu in the area? Did the chap who used the paint-pot not follow these directions?

Michiton Oladabas

The last document's final page offers an intriguing hint of what the document could be about. On the upper right hand corner, which is written in a faint manner and the vellum stained by the countless dirty hands, are lines of text that appear be written in Latin and some Voynich words scattered throughout. To understand these words, it is helpful if you're an expert on documents from the medieval period and familiar with the letters in different forms in that period. But even experts cannot determine what's being said here. The first two phrases on the second line appear to be "Michiton Oladabas" to me. What would you say?

A specialist in writing from the medieval period, Johannes Albus, deciphered the text in this manner (abbreviations and omissions within Square brackets):

poxleber umen[do] putriter.

+ an[te] chiton olei dabas + multas + t[un]c + t[an]ta[a](?) cer[a]e + portas + M[ixtura] +

fix[a+ man[nipulis] + mor[sulis] vix plus alt[e]ra + mature

... ... (two encrypted words) pals [ein]en pbrey nim[m] gei[s]smi[l]ch

The translation he used was:

Billy goat's liver is used for wet Rot

On the membrane, you give oil, you then bring lots of the(?) wax, which is in a

fixed mix 9 hands full nine morsels (from) the only double mature

... ... (two words that are ciphered) Squash to form a smooth paste then drink goat's milk.

The question here is why this plaintext is difficult to comprehend. There are two words that are enciphered in the fourth line appears to provide a fantastic narrator into the cipher. How difficult would it be to determine what these two words are in their context in the plaintext? Evidently, it's very difficult to say ...

Plaintext on F17r

There is a third place in the Manuscript which contains writing that appears as if it is plaintext: there's an unreadable line of text in the upper right-hand corner in Folio 17r.

It appears to read (if you are able to squint enough): "malhar allar lut3 the best vitellum" ... with possibly some small characters later. (Incidentally, Pelling examined this the folio in UV light and noticed evidence of Voynich symbols at the conclusion of the phrase.) What could this suggest? Let's take each word individually:

1. malhar - (Portugese) meaning "strike" or "thresh"

2. allar - (Icelandic) meaning "all"

3."lut3" 3. lut3 (Latin) Luteum meaning "yellow". The line of text that appears just above "t3" is macron. Scribes in the Middle Ages typically employed it to signify an abbreviation. It is usually an absence of "m" and "n". The "3" could also refer to an absence of "ue".

4. best - (English) meaning "best"

5. vitellum - (Latin) meaning "yolk"

The most likely interpretation is an enigmatic multi-language directive to "beat all of your best yellow yolks" Perhaps to create a dessert with the plants depicted on the same page? Is it possible that the person writing the instructions was writing down the recipe? Naturally, this interpretation and reading are extremely doubtful.